OTHER HELEN EXLEY GIFTBOOKS IN THIS SERIES:

A Feast of After Dinner Jokes   Old Wrecks' Jokes
A Portfolio of Business Jokes   A Spread of Over 40s' Jokes
A Megabyte of Computer Jokes   A Triumph of Over 50s' Jokes
A Century of Cricket Jokes   A Jubilee of Over 60s' Jokes
A Binge of Diet Jokes   A Knockout of Sports Jokes
A Round of Golf Jokes   A Bouquet of Wedding Jokes
A Romp of Naughty Jokes

Published simultaneously in 1999 by Exley Publications Ltd in
Great Britain, and Exley Publications LLC in the USA.
Arrangement and selection copyright © Helen Exley 1999
Text copyright © Stuart and Linda Macfarlane 1999
Cartoons copyright © Bill Stott 1999
The moral right of the author has been asserted.

12 11 10 9 8 7 6 5 4

Written by Stuart and Linda Macfarlane.
Cartoons by Bill Stott.
Edited by Claire Lipscomb.
Series Editor: Helen Exley.

ISBN 1-86187-123-6

A copy of the CIP data is available from the British Library on request.

Printed in Hungary.

Exley Publications Ltd, 16 Chalk Hill, Watford, Herts WD19 4BG, UK.
Exley Publications LLC, 232 Madison Avenue, Suite 1409, NY 10016, USA.
www.helenexleygiftbooks.com

OVER 30s'
JOKES

BY STUART & LINDA MACFARLANE
CARTOONS BY BILL STOTT

EXLEY
NEW YORK • WATFORD, UK

The dreaded day

Good Morning! Happy Birthday! No, all that praying during the night has not worked and the "Dreaded Day" has dawned. Get up *slowly*.
Remember your age.
Try to face the latter days of your life with some dignity.

Let there be singing and dancing in the street. It's fiesta time. It's your birthday.
Hurrah you're thirty!
... Thirty?
Let there be silence and calm in the street. It's siesta time. It's your thirtieth birthday.

Ways to mark your thirtieth birthday

- Light a bonfire – it's more environmentally friendly than burning all those candles.

- Try bungy jumping – bring the bridge down.

- Have a party – but only invite old, ugly friends.

- Work – after all you've wasted the rest of your life doing that.

- Sleep – you need plenty of beauty sleep at this age.

- Hide away.

THESE TWO TIMES 15!

Doomsday

"This is crazy," protested Jill to her friend. "I sympathize with you about turning thirty next week – but insisting everyone wears black to your party is just ridiculous."

"OK! OK?"

There is no need to feel miserable on your thirtieth birthday – there's a whole decade ahead for that.

How to spot a thirty year old man

- He uses a Jaguar key ring for his family saloon.
- He wears trousers that are too tight because he can't accept that the battle of the bulge is lost.
- He sports a beard – it's the only place where hair will grow.
- His zits have gone but the insecurity lingers on.
- His golf drive is bigger than his sex drive.
- He is constantly trying to chat up twenty year old women unsuccessfully.
- He's reading this book – but not laughing.

How to spot a thirty year old woman

- Her best friends are her hairdresser and beautician.
- She acts like a ten year old, dresses like a twenty year old and looks like a fifty year old.
- She applies her make-up with a trowel.
- She carries an extra handbag for her assorted wrinkle lotions.
- She has a bookshelf full of unopened diet and exercise books.
- She's reading this book and laughing – it describes all of her friends perfectly.

A wrinkly is born

Everyone remembers getting their first wrinkle. In horror we apply every anti-wrinkle lotion known to humanity.

But all to no avail, for the next day three new wrinkles appear and in sadness we accept the inevitable – we have joined the wrinklies club.

How wrinkly are you?

a. I'm not – my skin is as smooth as a baby's bottom.

b. With the help of some creams my wrinkles are under control.

c. I've been offered a part in a prune commercial.

How to deal with wrinkles

- Buy soft focus lenses for all your friends' spectacles.
- Fit rose-tinted mirrors in your house.
- A balaclava should hide most of those irritating little pleats.
- Get twenty hours beauty sleep per day.
- Become a creature of the night.

Downhill from here...

The first Saturday night following Gary's thirtieth birthday found him feeling lonely and depressed. All his younger friends were out clubbing and partying but for some reason that did not appeal to him.

In an effort to cheer himself up he decided he would phone some of his older friends whom he had not seen for a while. He thought of phoning Bill. But no, Bill only ever talked about his two young children. He couldn't call Ross because he spent every Saturday train spotting and David would be at his art class.

Of course... there was Jack. Gary had always found him incredibly boring because he was such a fanatical stamp collector. Gary reached for the phone, "Hello Jack, can I come round and see your stamps?"

"HE JUST KEEPS MUTTERING, IT'S ALL DOWNHILL FROM HERE...."

Thoughts on thirty

When you turn thirty, you discover for the first time that the volume control knob on your CD player turns to the left.

Thirty is when...

... washing your hair becomes a meaningless ritual to fill long lonely evenings.

... you start to take an interest in gardening.

... the parts of your past, which were so boring at the time, are now remembered with great sentiment.

... you use clothes to cover up rather than to reveal.

LITTLE BLACK DRESS R.I.P

At thirty a strange transformation takes place in the music lobe of the brain. Mysteriously this causes you to sing along with affection to songs you hated ten years earlier. In extreme cases you will even find yourself performing them at karaoke nights.

After thirty you are more likely to arrange to meet friends at a museum than a nightclub.

Thirty is when your collection of fitness videos outnumbers your movie videos.

CLOTHES THAT MAKE BUMS SMALL!

Desperately seeking...

It's hard to believe that in our early twenties we were so choosy about the people we dated! Did they have their own car? Did they have zits? Did they wear fashionable clothes? One small imperfection and they were told to get lost. Now, if anyone accidentally collides with our cart in the supermarket we pester them for their phone number.

The five stages of thirty-something courtship

1. Look for a willing partner.
2. Search relentlessly for a willing partner.
3. Hunt desperately for a willing partner.
4. Engage FBI's help in searching for a willing partner.
5. Abandon hope of ever finding a willing partner.

"WOW! RETRO-DANCING! I LOVE IT!"

Who is the fairest?

Learn to grow old gracefully – only scream and cry about your lost beauty, when you are all alone.

As your body begins to sag and wilt there are three stages in keeping your ego intact:

1. Trying to convince yourself that you look young.

2. Trying to fool your friends that you look young.

3. Trying to describe to the plastic surgeon the miracle that you would like them to perform to make you look young.

A physical write-off

During your thirties you face the predicament of keeping fit despite having no energy for serious exercise. A compromise must be found. There are two revolutionary forms of exercise:

Toe-aerobics: This involves lying on a bed and gently stretching the toes back and forward for five minutes each morning.

Mouth-callisthenics: Slowly curl the sides of the lips upwards and hold in that position for a few moments. (Exercise otherwise known as *smiling*.)

Warning: Overdoing these exercises can be harmful to your health.

EXERCISE:
A strenuous activity
such as reaching for
the remote control.
Avoid.

At thirty you swap the forty pushups
you did every morning
for an extra forty winks of sleep.

How do you spot a thirty-something
at the gymnasium?
They're the one collecting money at
the ticket office.

She says she is twenty-nine BUT...

... that means she must have married at thirteen.

... it's a hereditary condition – her mother claims to be thirty-nine.

... she changed to the Gregorian Calendar when she turned twenty.

... she was born on the twenty-ninth of February.

... she also says she's a natural blonde.

... her younger sister is thirty-five.

... she's got a phobia about big numbers.

... her watch stopped working for a few years.

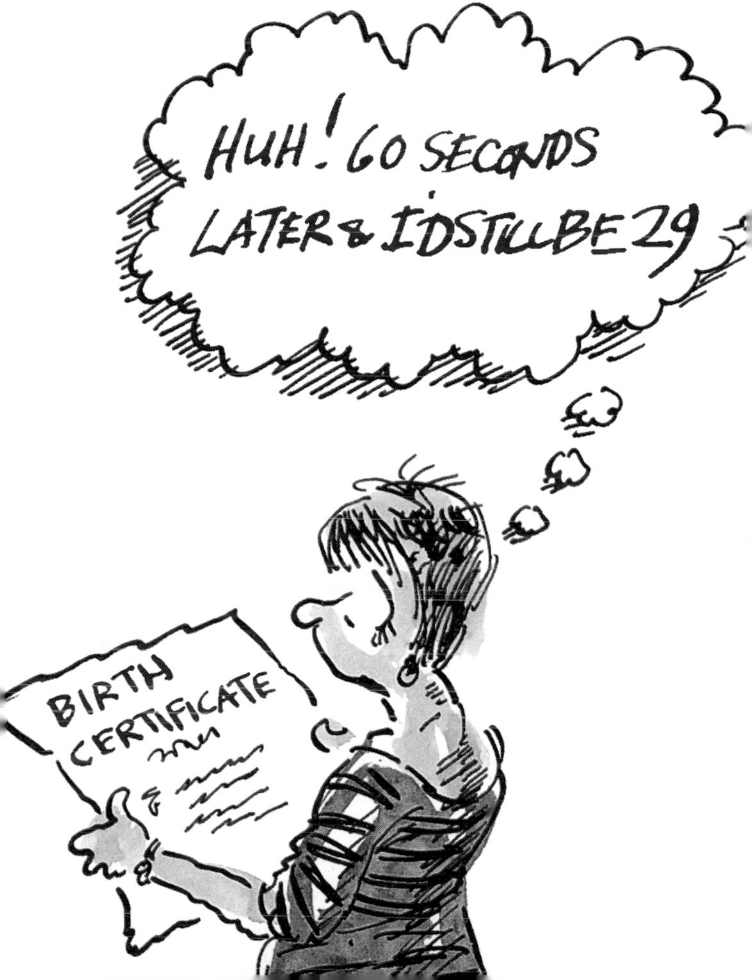
HUH! 60 SECONDS LATER & I'D STILL BE 29
BIRTH CERTIFICATE

The party's over

Don't worry. Your thirtieth birthday is just like any other day in your life. Which, now you've joined the thirty-somethings, means dreary, monotonous and pointless.

In your twenties you are often awake in the middle of the night enjoying sex or parties. In your thirties you are often awake in the middle of the night mourning the lack of sex and parties.

For a thirty-something "living life on the edge" is deciding whether to have pizza or pasta for dinner.

If you think that you're in your prime during your thirties then your twenties must have been unbelievably boring.

"SO YOU'RE THIRTY! NOW SHUT UP. YOU'RE RUINING JERRY SPRINGER!"

Signs of decrepitude

- You no longer have any desire or cause to celebrate your birthday.

- You don't have too much trouble bending down – it's getting up again that's the problem.

- Someone keeps putting white hairs in your hairbrush.

- Your dental bills are larger than your grocery bills.

- Your wrinkles develop wrinkles of their own.

- The glass in your spectacles becomes so thick that you need a counterbalance to wear them.

- Even wonderbras can't give you a lift.

- You become aware that the print size in books and magazines has started to get smaller.

"OH COME ON! BEING THIRTY'S NOT SO BAD. I ALWAYS THOUGHT YOU WERE FIFTY!"

Fashion disasters

At thirty you have reached the age when your taste in clothes changes with your size – not with fashion.

In your thirties you become convinced that clothing manufacturers are conspiring against you by changing all the size labels on their garments.

Many over-thirties just can't give up the habit of buying trendy clothes. They can be spotted in changing rooms, their curses audible over the rasping sound of splitting fabric.
Fortunately we are spared the tragic sight of these tortured souls in their vulgar attire, because at their age they never go anywhere.

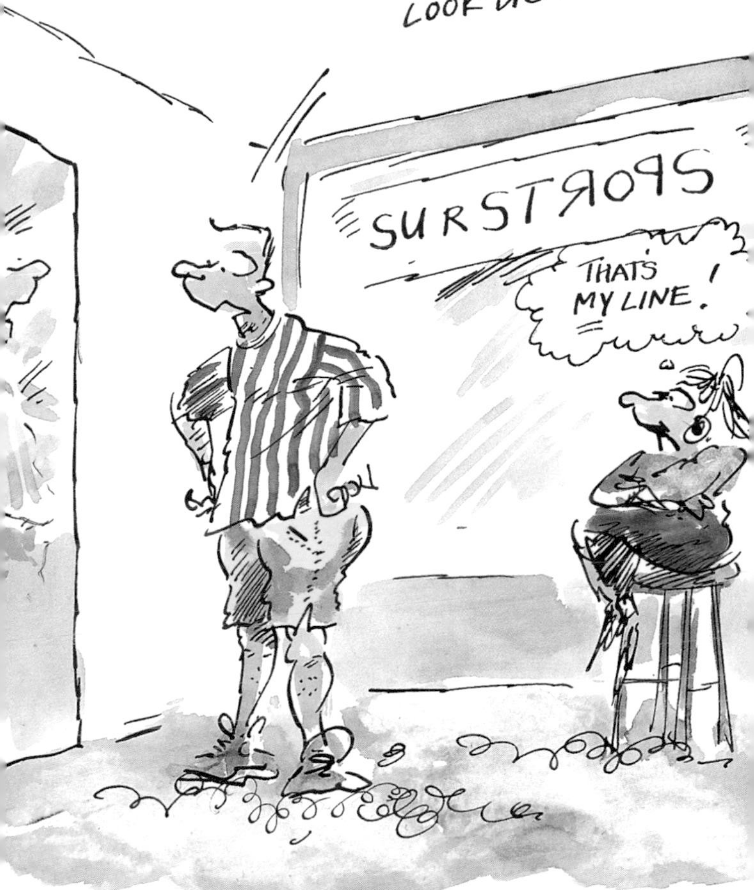

DOES MY BUM LOOK BIG IN THESE?

The over thirties' glossary

OH, NO! ONLY 40 YEARS LEFT!

LOVE: A transient state of mind when logic and reason are abandoned.
Condition is temporary.
Occurs less frequently with age.
Men often confuse it with lust.

SEX: An act most frequently performed alone. When performed with a partner it is purely for their pleasure as you would rather be sleeping or watching television. Anticipation always better than the act.

YOUTH: A far off mystical land populated by undeserving idiots. There are no roads leading IN to this land, only OUT of it.

HAPPINESS: A state somewhere between sadness and downright misery.

HOPE: see *Abandon*.

AMBITION: A burning desire for the status quo to continue for as long as possible.

MIDDLE AGE: A blasphemous expression.

Ten survival tips for your thirties

1. Take up hobbies to keep you active – for example, tiddlywinks and dominoes.

2. Dine by candlelight to conceal facial creases.

3. Master the ability to lie about your age without blushing.

4. Bed before ten o'clock.

5. No alcohol.

6. Strict calorie-controlled diet.

7. Sex no more than once a week.

8. No chocolate.

9. No activities which might cause excitement.

10. Above all – BE HAPPY!!!

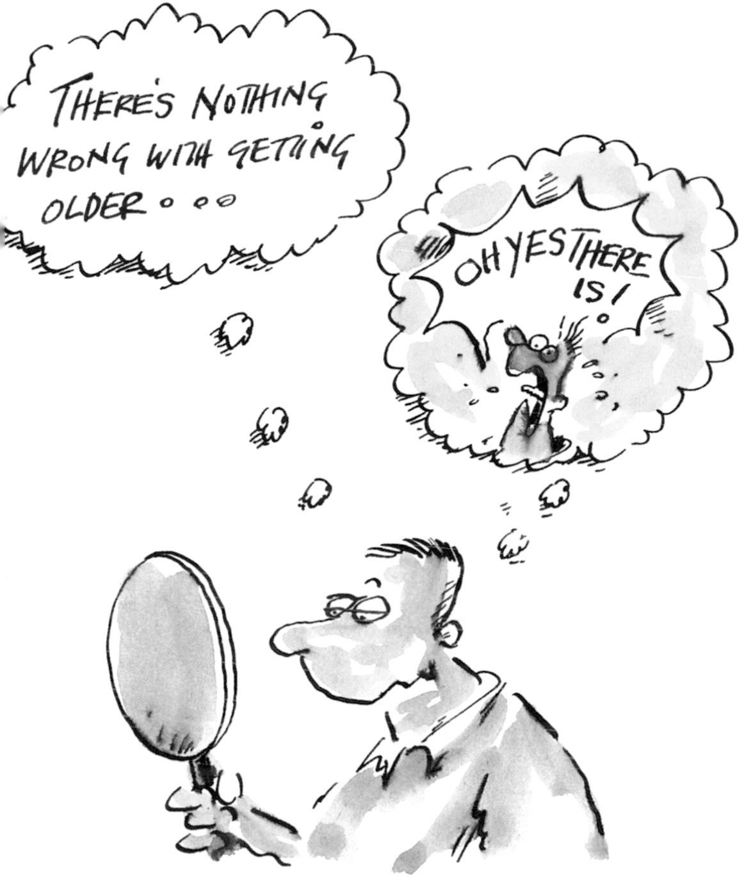
THERE'S NOTHING WRONG WITH GETTING OLDER . . . .
OH YES THERE IS!

In your prime

Past thirty? You are now in your prime. The opposite sex will find you irresistible. So put on your cardigan, slacks and slippers and prepare to be hunted.

Admit it, now that you're a thirty-something your chance of having sex is even less than the likelihood of being abducted by aliens and made ruler of their planet – pretty low!
In statistical terms the probability of you having sex with someone you find desirable:

$$= \frac{(\text{Their Age x Your Lust})}{(\text{Your Age x Their Loathing})} \times 0$$

In case the battery in your solar powered calculator has failed, the answer equals ZERO.

"YOU'RE AT LEAST THIRTY, AREN'T YOU? I MEAN
NOBODY DRINKS FROM THE BOTTLE ANY MORE...."

Going to pot

As you enter your thirties you will need to find ways to avoid getting a massive pot-belly. Going on crash diets and taking copious amounts of exercise will help. As a precaution replace all your clothes with larger sizes.

In your thirties many new doors will open giving you great opportunities for success, wealth and happiness. Unfortunately, because of that pot-belly, you will be unable to get through.

Uses for a droopy tummy

- Take a job in a department store as an all year round Santa.

- Make use of it as a portable shelf.

- Use it to keep the rain off your feet.

- Tattoo flowers on your tummy and enjoy watching them grow as your waistline expands.

- Use it as a bumper when you collide with the furniture.

Over thirty at work

You have always shown great enthusiasm, worked long hours and put the company's interests before your own.

Now, however, you reap the rewards for all your sacrifices.

The first indication is that the office junior is promoted and becomes your boss. After a brief meeting to reassure you that you are still a valuable member of the team, your computer is replaced by a calculator, your office is relocated in the goods elevator, and you are sent on job rehabilitation to learn how to make coffee.

As the ultimate accolade you are given the option of very early retirement or relocation to the company's satellite branch three hundred miles away. In jubilation you accept the latter – this is the career opportunity you have been striving for all along.

"I'M THIRTY. I STILL HAVEN'T WON THE LOTTERY OR
STARRED IN A BLOCKBUSTER MOVIE. AND I'M
GETTING A PAUNCH! THIS CAN'T BE FAIR!"

Feeling broody

Now that you are in your thirties the question of children is sure to arise. There are some excellent reasons why you should have children:

a. you are both getting old

b. all your friends are starting families

c. your parents are sending threatening letters demanding grandchildren.

There are also arguments against:

a. you are poverty stricken

b. children are a burden for the next twenty years

c. you hate children.

So, that's it settled then – you order a buggy, a crib, and start choosing names.

The bald truth

The probability of your toupee falling off is directly proportional to the attractiveness of the person you are trying to impress.

Ninety-nine percent of toupees are discarded in disgust and humiliation within a month of purchase. Rather than throw yours away, recycle it as a mop, a bird's nest or a winter jacket for a Chihuahua.

A simple method of hiding your withering hair is to shave it all off. This can make you look much younger – provided your head is not covered in wrinkles.

"BALD SPOT!? WHAT DO YOU MEAN, BALD SPOT?"

Sex

In your thirties sex becomes something special, something cherished – not a trivial event that happens in the back seats of cars. Rather than many fleeting romantic encounters, sex is kept for important occasions – such as the discovery of a new planet.

Thirty-somethings have bedtime headaches much more frequently than when in their twenties. Not the kind of headaches that stop them reading a novel or watching TV in bed.

"We're all set for a wild night of passion"
declared Sandra, to her husband,
as she entered the bedroom. "I've got
everything we need, cocoa, Viagra...
and your headache tablets."

"LOOK THERE HE GOES... THIRTY-ONE, AND BOUGHT HIS FIRST PACK OF VIAGRA!"

Battling the bulge

DIET: A method of reducing food intake without eating less. Always performed at a future date – usually tomorrow.

A common war cry of the thirty-something is, "I'm on a diet." This expression can mean anything from, "I intend starting a diet", to "I've gone two hours without eating a box of chocolates."

In your thirties, you may find it helpful to remember the two invariable laws of dieting:

1. The harder and longer you diet the greater your weight gain will be.
2. For every kilo your best friend loses you will gain two.

"PREPARE TO MEET THY DOOM!"

Advice for friends of the over thirties

- Never give a birthday card with an age on it.
- Do not mention their age in public unless you know what age they are pretending to be.
- Respect their feelings, "ignore" their birthday.

- Never say "you're looking good" – this merely emphasizes that they have entered the age of decline.

- Cover all mirrors – every glance is a blow to their ego.

- Never ask how the latest diet is going – the answer is obvious.

Prepare for old age

Now that you're in your thirties you'll have to redefine all those adjectives you used for people of such advanced years. So for "boring" use *dynamic*, for "old" use *mature* and for "old-fashioned" use *sophisticated*.

Every thirty-something should seriously consider taking out a retirement plan for their old age. This is the strategy of being impoverished and miserable now, so that you have money to spend when you are incapable of enjoying it.

The Kalmer Sutra

In your thirties you need to take a more laid back approach to lovemaking. Here are some positions to try:

The Tête-à-Tête: In this position the couple lie side by side and simultaneously complain of headaches.

The Zzzz: Action postponed until morning.

The Snatch: A ten minute cuddle while the baby sleeps.

The Missionary: The couple pray for deliverance.

The Chiller: After ten minutes a break is taken to have an ice-cream.

The Frenzy: This position requires some movement and should only be undertaken after a full medical check up.

Hand holding is optional in these positions.

NB: Should none of these positions appeal, don't despair. During your thirties you will discover things that don't even get a mention in the *Kamasutra*... like woodcarving, antique collecting, origami....

"QUICK! SING SOMETHING – I'M LOSING MY RHYTHM!"

29 forever

When a woman tells you her age add on five years to get her true age.
To be popular, subtract five years from her actual age and tell her this is how old she looks.

Lie detectors have been used effectively to convict murderers, international jewel thieves and hardened hit men. However, when attempting to establish a woman's age they are woefully inadequate.

"HE SAID IT WAS TOO YOUNG FOR ME. SO I SLUGGED
HIM. I'LL TAKE IT."

Some advantages of being over thirty

- You can now afford all the things you no longer want.

- You no longer blush when you chat up members of the opposite sex – because you no longer chat up members of the opposite sex.

- You have lots of spare time in which to read your junk mail.

- For the first time you are able to count all the hairs on your head.

- When watching TV you can irritate others by telling them the endings to all those old films you saw first time round.

- You can eat as much as you wish and blame the consequences on middle age spread.

Goals to achieve by my thirtieth birthday

Learn to fly a plane.

Go right to the top of the company.

Become a star – world famous!

Sail single-handed round world.

Have a major exhibition of my artwork.

Make a positive contribution to world peace.